Seasonal

Runner Quilts

Dress Your Tables for Any Seasons

DEDICATION

Contents

Center Pieces

Create a table runner in no time with precut strips left over from another project and chain piecing.

Materials

11—2-1/2x42" precut strips assorted prints (table runner center)

1-1/8 yards yellow print (border, binding)

2-1/4 yards backing fabric

28×80" batting

Finished table runner: 20×72"

Yardages and cutting instructions are based on 42" of usable fabric width. Measurements include 1/4" seam allowances. Sew with right sides together unless otherwise stated.

Cut Fabrics

Cut pieces in the following order.

From yellow print, cut:

4—4-1/4×42" strips for border

5—2-1/2×42" binding strips

2—4-1/4×12-1/2" border strips

Assemble Table Runner Center

For the featured table runner, designer used the technique known as the "Jelly Roll Race."

1) Using diagonal seams, join assorted print 2-1/2×42" strips along short edges to make a pieced strip about 440" long (Diagram 1). Trim seam allowances to 1/4" and press seams open.

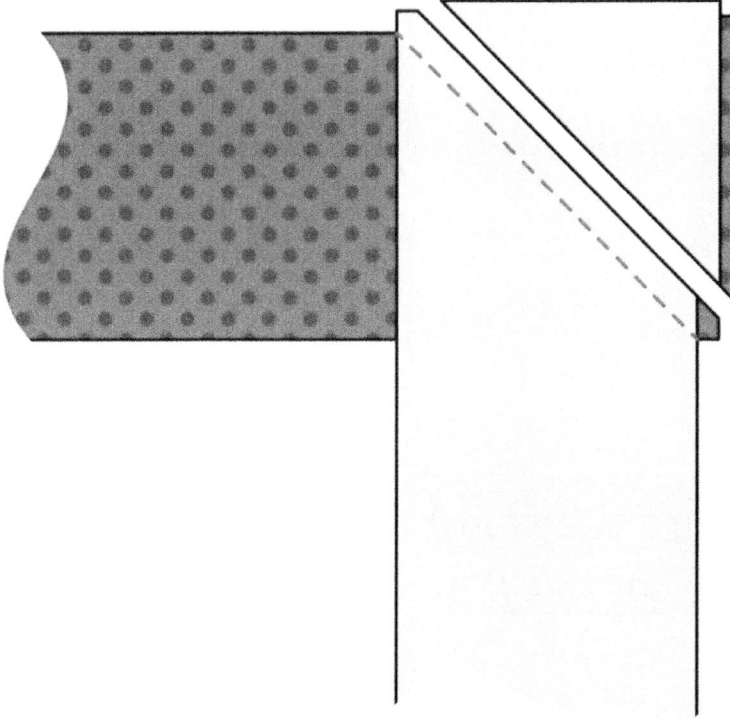

DIAGRAM 1

2) Cut an 18"-long strip from one end of pieced strip (this allows seams to offset each other as table runner center is assembled).

3) With right side inside, fold pieced strip in half, matching short raw

3

edges. Sew together along one long edge, stopping 1/4" from fold (Diagram 2). Slip a scissors inside fold and cut pieced strip in half. Open pieces to make a 4-1/2×211" strip (Diagram 3).

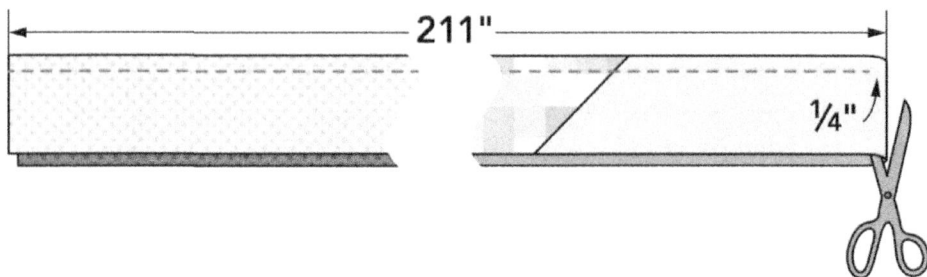

DIAGRAM 2

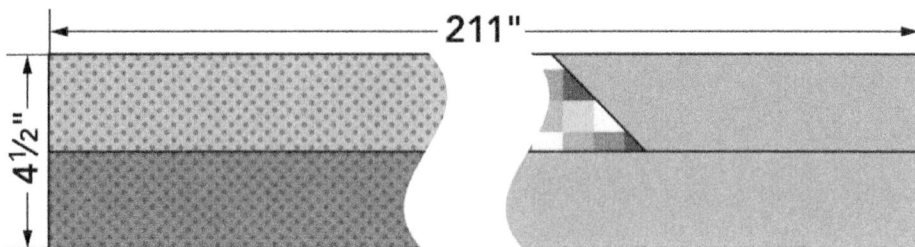

DIAGRAM 3

4) Fold 4-1/2×211" strip in half as before, matching short raw ends. Sew and cut as before to make an 8-1/2×105-1/2" strip.

5) Repeat the folding, sewing, and cutting process a total of five times to make a pieced unit. Press seams in one direction. The unit should be approximately 13×64-1/2" including seam allowances. Trim pieced unit to 12-1/2×64-1/2" including seam allowances to make table

runner center.

Add Border

1) Join yellow print 4-1/4×12-1/2" border strips to short edges of table runner center (Table Runner Assembly Diagram). Press seams toward border.

2) Cut and piece yellow print 4-1/4×42" strips to make:

2—4-1/4×72" border strips

3) Add 4-1/4×72" border strips to remaining edges to complete table runner top. Press seams toward border.

Finish Table Runner

1) Layer table runner top, batting, and backing; baste.

2) Quilt as desired. Clarine Howe machine-quilted five-petal flowers and swirls across the table runner top.

3) Bind with yellow print binding strips.

Seasonal Table Runner Quilts

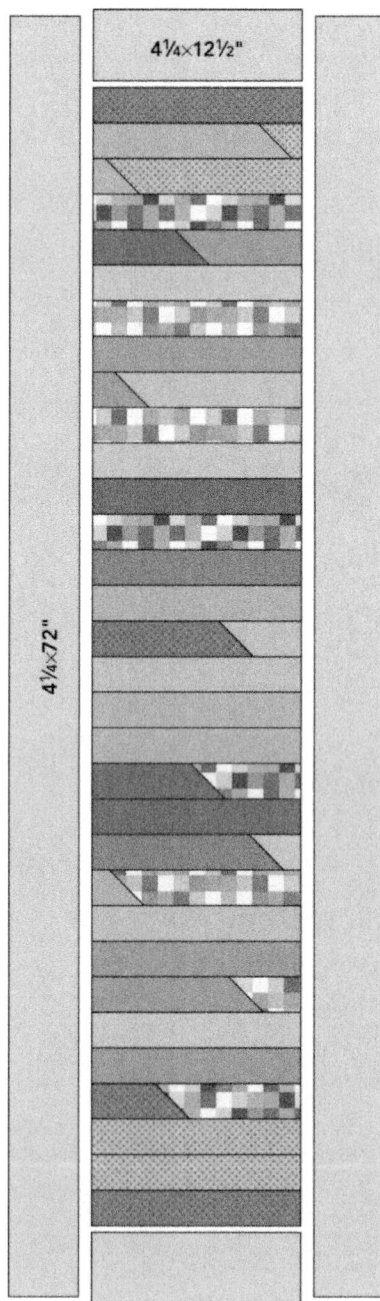

4¼×12½"

4¼×72"

TABLE RUNNER ASSEMBLY DIAGRAM

Square Scramble

Seasonal Table Runner Quilts

A quick-to-piece table runner and coordinating place mats in a calming color combo add interest to an inviting tabletop.

Materials

1/2 yard white-and-tan print (blocks)

18×21" piece (fat quarter)gold stripe (blocks)

9×21" piece (fat eighth) tan-and-white print (blocks)

18×21" piece (fat quarter) green medallion print (blocks)

9×21" piece (fat eighth) green spiral print (blocks)

18×21" piece (fat quarter) tan doodle print (blocks)

18×21" piece (fat quarter) tan spiral print (blocks)

1-1/4 yards tan medallion print (place mat side units, borders, binding)

2-1/2 yards backing fabric

23×59" rectangle batting for table runner 2—20×25" rectangles batting for place mats

Finished Place Mat: 14-1/2×19-1/2"

Finished Table Runner: 14-1/2×50-1/2"

Finished Block: 12" square

Yardages and cutting instructions are based on 42" of usable fabric width.

Measurements include 1/4" seam allowances. Sew with right sides together unless otherwise stated.

Press seams in directions indicated by arrows on diagrams. If no direction is specified, press seams toward darker fabric.

Cut Fabrics

Cut pieces in the following order.

From white-and-tan print, cut:

2—2×12-1/2" rectangles

4—1-1/2×12-1/2" rectangles

6—3-1/2×6-1/2" rectangles

6—3-1/2" squares

From gold stripe, cut:

12—3-1/2" squares

From tan-and-white print, cut:

6—3-1/2" squares

From green medallion print, cut:

6—3-1/2×6-1/2" rectangles

6—3-1/2" squares

From green spiral print, cut:

6—3-1/2" squares

From tan doodle print, cut:

6—3-1/2×6-1/2" rectangles

6—3-1/2" squares

From tan spiral print, cut:

6—3-1/2×6-1/2" rectangles

6—3-1/2" squares

From tan medallion print, cut:

8—2-1/2×42" binding strips

3—1-1/2×42" strips for border of table runner

4—1-1/2×19-1/2" border strips for place mats

2—1-1/2×14-1/2" border strips for table runner

4—1-1/2×12-1/2" border strips for place mats

4—1-1/4×12-1/2" rectangles

From backing fabric, cut:

1—23×59" rectangle

2—20×25" rectangles

Assemble blocks

1) Sew together one white-and-tan print 3-1/2" square and one gold stripe 3-1/2" square (Diagram 1).

2) Aligning long edges, add a white-and-tan print 3-1/2×6-1/2"

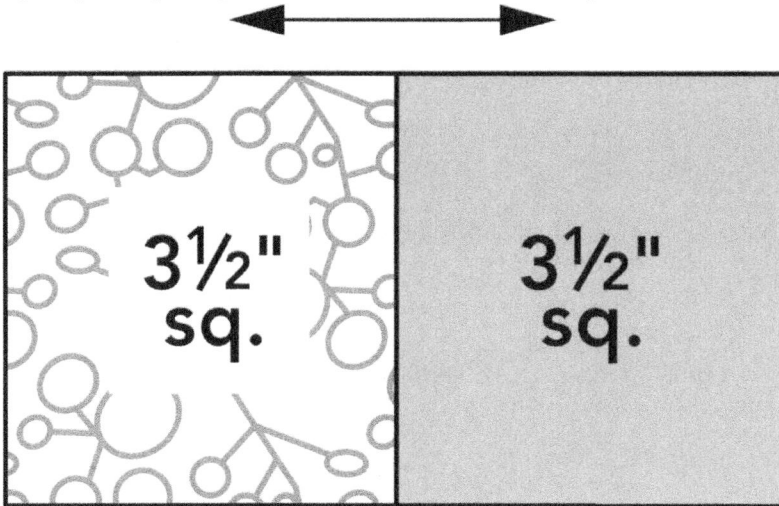

DIAGRAM 1

11

rectangle to Step 1 segment to make Unit A (Diagram 2). Unit A should be 6-1/2" square including seam allowances.

3) Repeat steps 1 and 2 to make six A units total.

4) Using tan-and-white print 3-1/2" squares and green medallion print 3-1/2" squares and 3-1/2×6-1/2" rectangles, repeat steps 1 and 2 to make six B units (Diagram 2).

5) Using green spiral print 3-1/2" squares and tan doodle print 3-1/2" squares and 3-1/2×6-1/2" rectangles, repeat steps 1 and 2 to make six C units (Diagram 2).

6) Using gold stripe 3-1/2" squares and tan spiral print 3-1/2" squares and 3-1/2×6-1/2" rectangles, repeat steps 1 and 2 to make six D units (Diagram 2).

7) Sew together one each of A, B, C, and D units in pairs. Join pairs to make a block. The block should be 12-1/2" square including seam allowances.

8) Repeat Step 7 to make six blocks total.

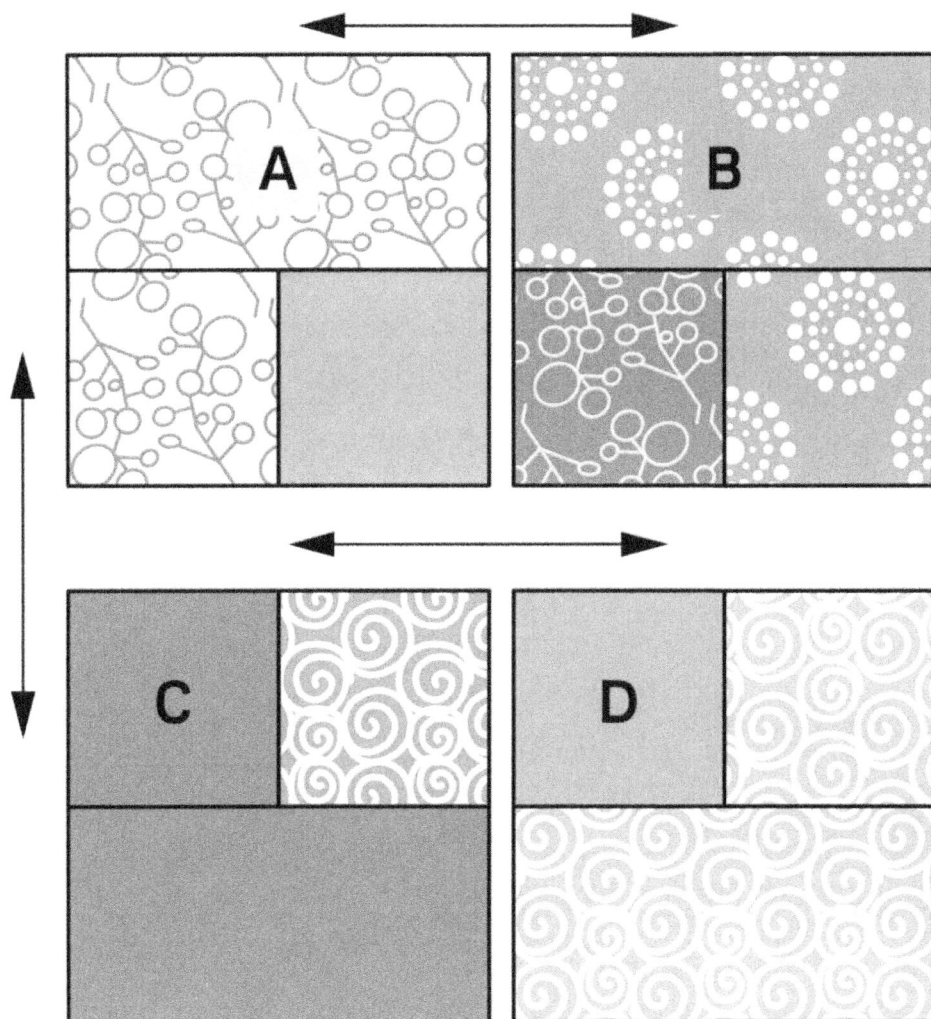

DIAGRAM 2

Assemble Place Mat Tops

1) Referring to Diagram 3, sew together one white-and-tan print 2×12-

1/2" rectangle, two tan medallion print 1-1/4×12-1/2" rectangles, and two white-and-tan print 1-1/2×12-1/2" rectangles to make a side unit. Press seams toward tan medallion print rectangles. The unit should be 5-1/2×12-1/2" including seam allowances.

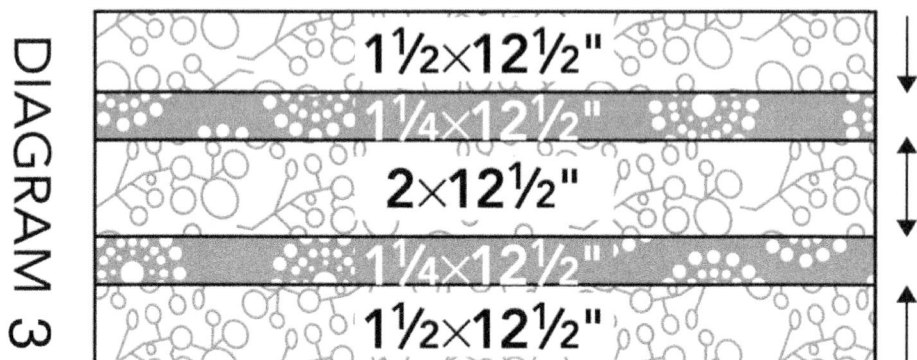

DIAGRAM 3

1½×12½"
1¼×12½"
2×12½"
1¼×12½"
1½×12½"

2) Add side unit to left-hand edge of a block to make place mat center. Press seam toward side unit. The place mat center should be 12-1/2×17-1/2" including seam allowances.

3) Referring to Place Mat Assembly Diagram, join tan medallion print 1-1/2×12-1/2" border strips to short edges of place mat center. Add tan medallion print 1-1/2×19-1/2" border strips to remaining edges to make place mat top. Press all seams toward border.

4) Repeat steps 1–3 to make a second place mat top.

1½×19½"

1½×12½"

PLACE MAT ASSEMBLY DIAGRAM

Assemble Table Runner Top

1) Referring to Table Runner Assembly Diagram, lay out remaining blocks in a row, rotating every other block 180°.

2) Sew together blocks to make table runner center. Press seams in one direction. The table runner center should be 12-1/2×48-1/2" including seam allowances.

1½×14½"

1½×48½"

TABLE RUNNER ASSEMBLY DIAGRAM

3) Sew together tan medallion print 1-1/2×42" strips to make 2—1-1/2×48-1/2"-long strips for border.

4) Sew tan medallion print 1-1/2×48-1/2" border strips to long edges of table runner center. Add tan medallion print 1-1/2×14-1/2" border strips to remaining edges to make table runner top. Press all seams toward border.

Finish Place Mats and Table Runner

1) Layer a place mat top, batting 20×25" rectangle, and backing 20×25" rectangle; baste.

2) Quilt as desired. Designer Kate Colleran machine-quilted a square spiral in the center four squares of each block and straight vertical lines about 3/8" apart in the remaining areas.

3) Bind with tan medallion print binding strips to complete place mat.

4) Repeat steps 1–3 to complete a second place mat.

5) Using table runner top, batting 23×59" rectangle, and backing 23×59" rectangle, repeat steps 1–3 to complete table runner.

On the Bright Side

Sew a bright table topper using precut print strips and solid white. The white makes the colors pop.

Seasonal Table Runner Quilts

Materials

1/2 yard solid white (blocks)

11--2-1/2x42" strips assorted prints in red, yellow, green, and blue (blocks)

4--2-1/2x42" strips green print (binding)

1-1/2 yards backing fabric

27×51" batting

Easy Angle ruler (optional)

Finished quilt: 18-1/2×42-1/2"

Finished block: 6" square

Yardages and cutting instructions are based on 42" of usable fabric width.

Measurements include 1/4" seam allowances. Sew with right sides together unless otherwise stated.

Press seams in directions indicated by arrows in diagrams. If no direction is indicated, press seams toward darker fabric.

Cut Fabrics

Cut pieces in the following order.

From solid white, cut:

88--2-1/2" squares or 44-2-1/2" squares and 44 triangles

From each assorted print strip, cut:

14--2-1/2" squares or 10-2-1/2" squares and 4 triangles

Assemble Churn Dash Blocks

1. Use a pencil to mark a diagonal line on wrong side of 44 solid white 2-1/2" squares. (To prevent fabric from stretching as you draw the lines, place 220-grit sandpaper under each square.)

2. Sew together a marked solid white square and an assorted print square on marked line. Trim seam allowance to 1/4". Press open attached triangle to make a triangle-square (Diagram 1). Repeat to make four matching triangle-squares total.

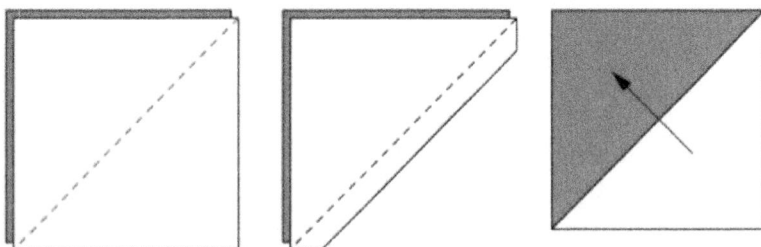

DIAGRAM 1

3. Repeat Step 2 to make 44 triangle-squares total (11 sets of four matching triangle-squares).

4. For one Churn Dash block, gather four matching triangle-squares, one matching print 2-1/2" square, and four solid white 2-1/2" squares.

5. Referring to Diagram 2, sew together Step 4 pieces in three horizontal rows. Join rows to make a Churn Dash block. The block should be 6-1/2" square including seam allowances.

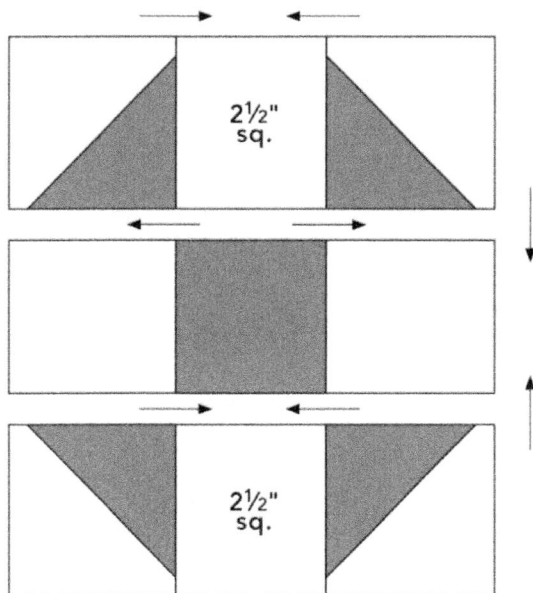

DIAGRAM 2

6. Repeat steps 4 and 5 to make 11 Churn Dash blocks total.

Assemble Nine-Patch Blocks

1. Referring to Diagram 3, sew together nine assorted print 2-1/2" squares in three horizontal rows. Join rows to make a Nine-Patch block. The block should be 6-1/2" square including seam allowances.

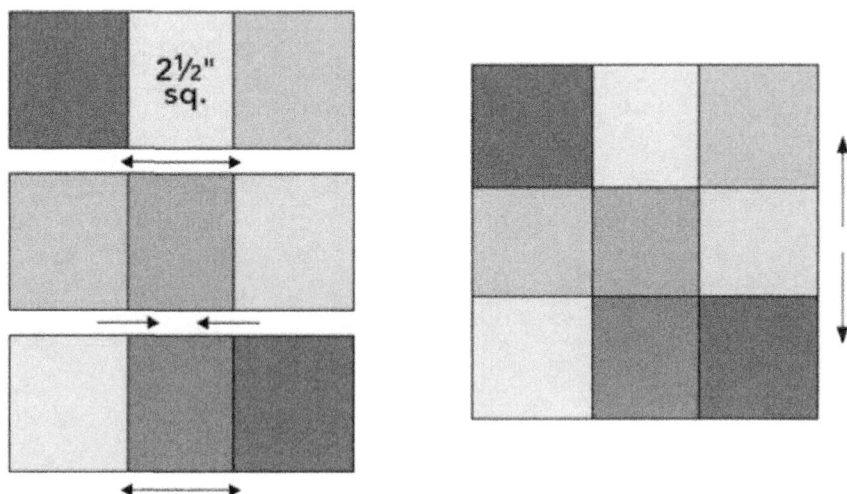

DIAGRAM 3

2. Repeat Step 1 to make 10 Nine-Patch blocks total. (You will have nine assorted print 2-1/2" squares left over.)

Assemble Quilt Top

1. Referring to Table Runner Assembly Diagram, alternate Churn Dash blocks and Nine-Patch blocks in seven horizontal rows.

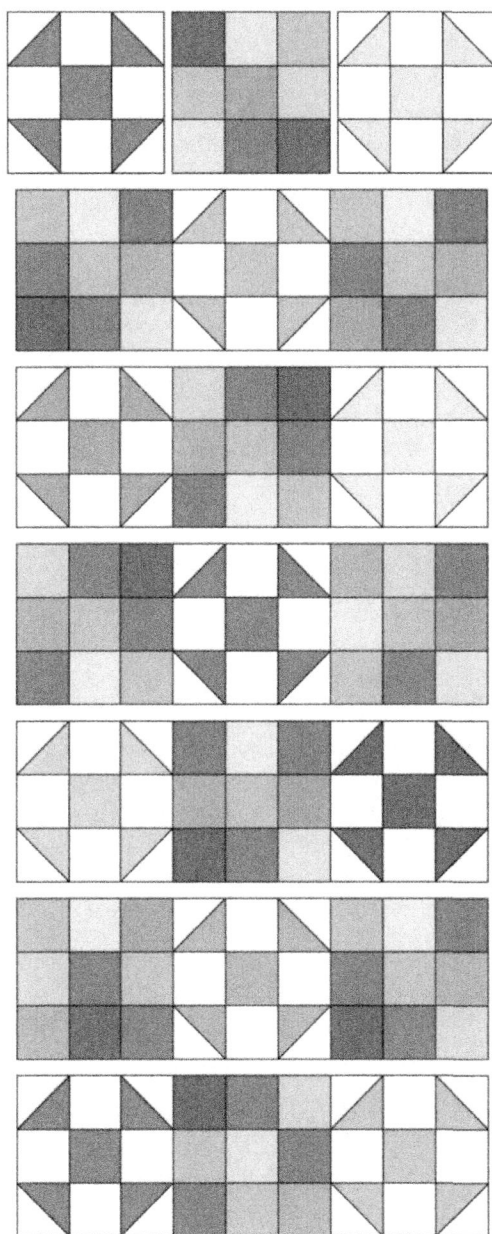

TABLE RUNNER ASSEMBLY DIAGRAM

23

2. Sew together pieces in each row. Press seams toward Churn Dash blocks.

3. Join rows to make quilt top; press seams in one direction. The quilt center should be 18-1/2×42-1/2" including seam allowances.

Finish Quilt

1. Layer quilt top, batting, and backing; baste. Quilt as desired.

2. Bind with green print binding strips.

Sunflower Table Runner

Scraps in vibrant colors unite in a table runner that's sure to bring cheer to any space.

Materials

Yardages and cutting instructions are based on 42" of usable fabric width.

3—10" squares in green floral, blue floral, and orange floral (blocks)

3—10" squares in green print, blue print, and orange print (blocks)

3—10" squares in green tone-on-tone, blue tone-on-tone, and orange tone-on-tone (blocks)

3—10" squares mottled green, mottled blue, and mottled orange (blocks)

1/4 yard yellow print (sashing, inner border)

1/2 yard blue sunflower print (outer border)

3/8 yard mottled dark blue (binding)

27×50" batting

1-1/2 yards backing fabric

FINISHED TABLE RUNNER: 19×42"

FINISHED BLOCK: 10-1/2" square

Cut Fabrics

Cut pieces in the following order.

From each assorted floral, cut:

1—3-1/2" square

4—2×3-1/2" rectangles

4—2" squares

From each assorted print, cut:

4—2×3-1/2" rectangles

From each assorted tone-on-tone, cut:

3—3-1/2" squares, cutting each diagonally twice in an X for 12 small triangles total

From each assorted mottled square, cut:

4—2×6-1/2" rectangles

2—3-1/2" squares, cutting each in half diagonally 4 large triangles total

From yellow print, cut:

2—1-1/2 ×34" inner border strips

2—1-1/2 ×13" inner border strips

2—1-1/2 ×11" sashing strips

From blue sunflower print, cut:

2—3-1/2×36" outer border strips

2—3-1/2×19" outer border strips

From mottled dark blue, cut:

4—2-1/2×42" binding strips

Assemble Blocks

Measurements include 1/4" seam allowances. Sew with right sides together unless otherwise stated.

Press seams in directions indicated by arrows on diagrams. If no direction is specified, press seam toward darker fabric.

1. Gather all green squares, rectangles, and triangles.

2. Referring to Diagram 1 (next page), lay out green floral 3-1/2" square, green floral 2" squares, and green print 2×3-1/2" rectangles. Sew together pieces in rows. Join rows to make block center. The block center should be 6-1/2" square including seam allowances.

3. Sew together two green tone-on-tone small triangles and one mottled green 2×6-1/2" rectangle to make Unit A. Repeat to make a second Unit A.

4. Sew together two green tone-on-tone small triangles and one green floral 2×3-1/2" rectangle to make Unit B. Repeat to make four B units total.

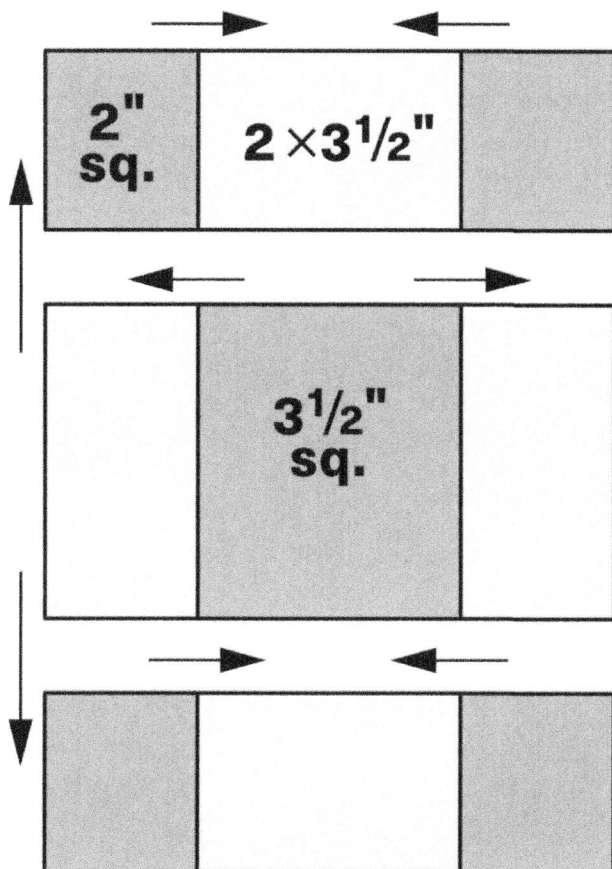

Diagram 1

5. Referring to Diagram 2, sew remaining mottled green 2×6-1/2" rectangles to opposite edges of block center. Add A units to remaining edges. Trim triangle points even with mottled rectangles.

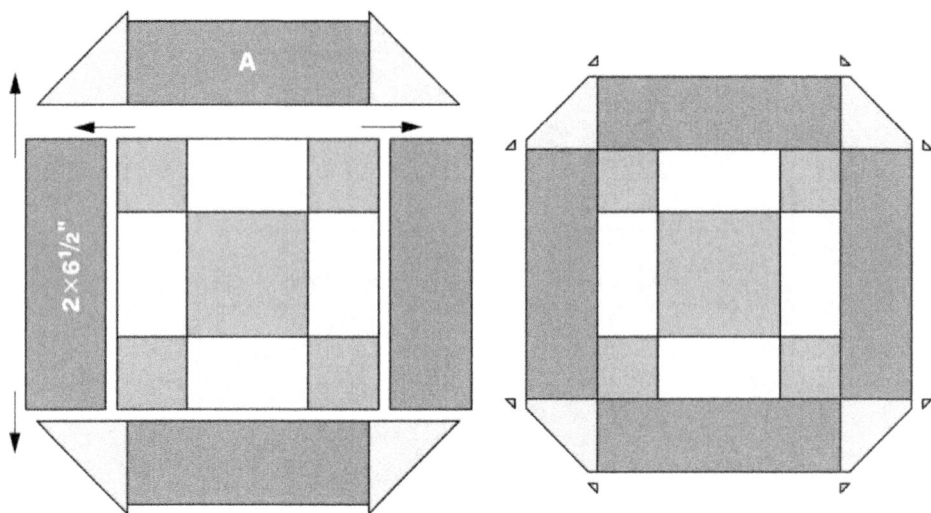

Diagram 2

6. Referring to Diagram 3, sew B units to Step 5 unit. Trim triangle points even with green floral rectangles.

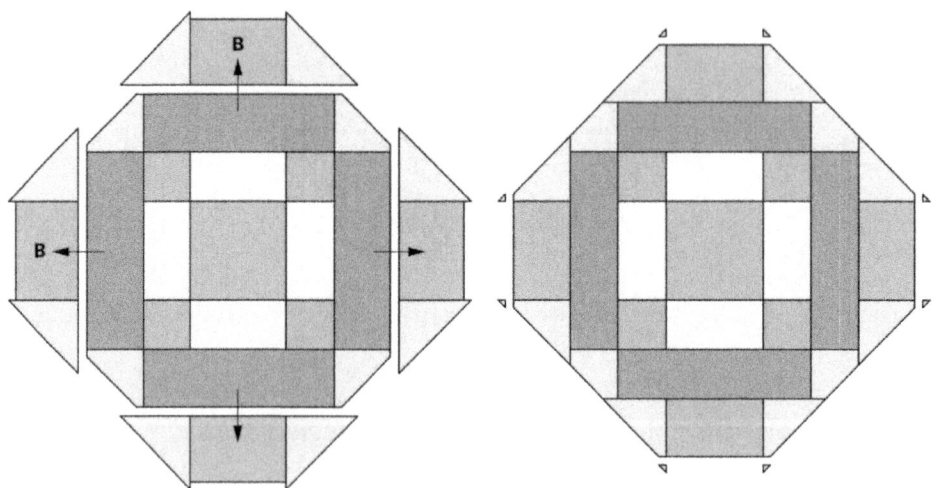

Diagram 3

7. Referring to Diagram 4, join mottled green large triangles to Step 6 unit to make a block. Measuring 1/4" from rectangle corners, trim block to 11" square including seam allowances.

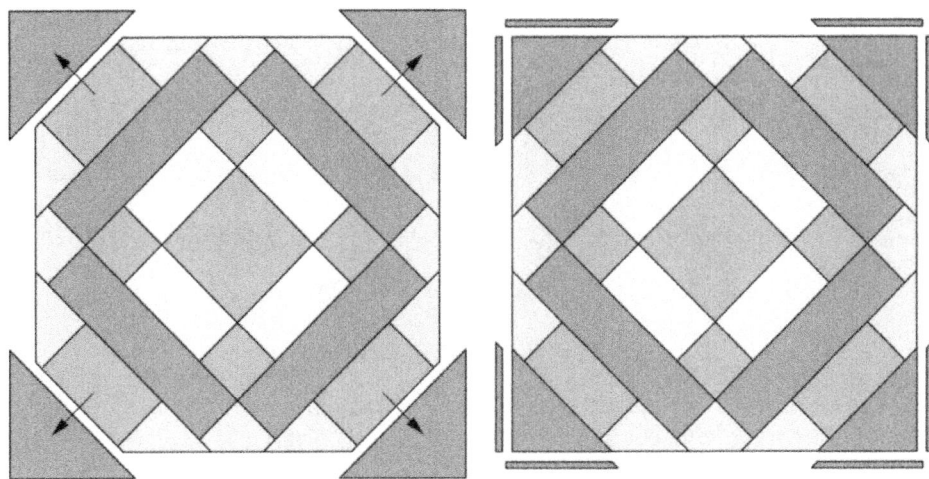

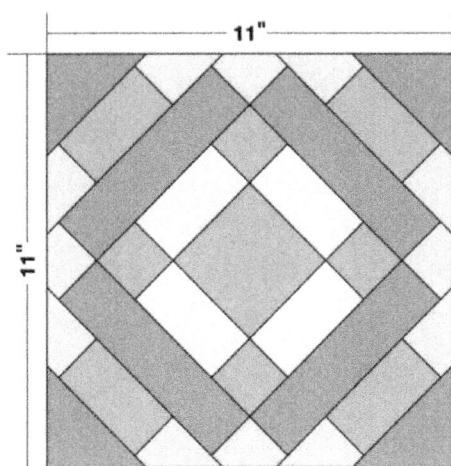

Diagram 4

8. Using blue squares, rectangles, and triangles and orange squares, rectangles, and triangles, repeat steps 1–7 twice to make a blue block and an orange block.

Assemble Table Runner Top

1. Referring to Table Runner Assembly Diagram, lay out blocks and yellow print 1-1/2×11" sashing strips in a row. Sew together pieces in row; press seams toward sashing strips to make quilt center. The quilt center should be 11×34" including seam allowances.

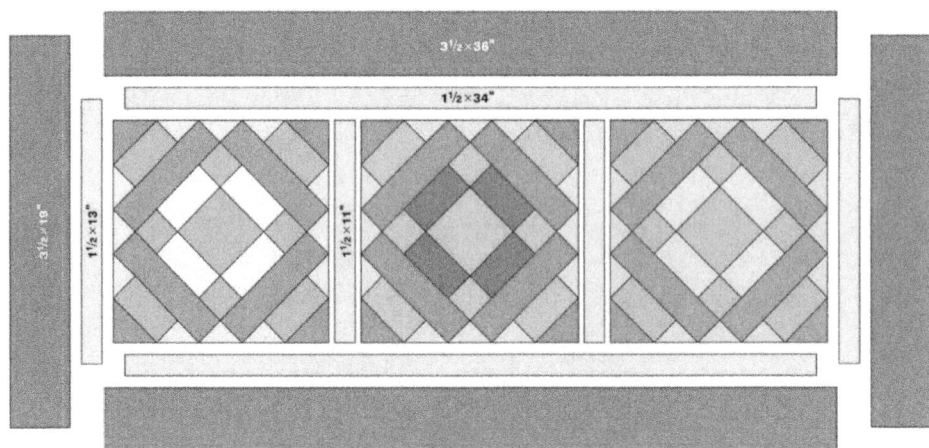

Table Runner Assembly Diagram

2. Sew yellow print 11/2×34" inner border strips to long edges of quilt center. Sew yellow print 11/2×13" inner border strips to remaining edges. Press seams towards inner border.

3. Sew blue sunflower print 3-1/2×36" outer border strips to long

32

edges of quilt center. Add blue sunflower print 3-1/2×19" outer border strips to remaining edges to complete quilt top. Press seams toward outer border.

Finish Table Runner

1. Layer table runner top, batting, and backing; baste. Quilt as desired.

2. Bind with mottled dark blue binding strips.

Fiesta Pinwheels

Seasonal Table Runner Quilts

Punch up your summer table with a runner that's easier than it looks. It's all about the fabric placement-we show you how!

Materials

1/3 yard yellow print (blocks)

1/3 yard solid cream (blocks)

1/3 yard red print (blocks)

1/3 yard green print (blocks)

1/3 yard blue print (blocks)

1/4 yard solid red (inner border)

1-5/8 yards blue-and-green stripe (outer border)

2/3 yard blue check (binding)

1-3/4 yards backing fabric

26×62" batting

Finished table runner: 17-1/2×53-1/2"

Finished block: 9" square

Quantities are for 44/45"-wide, 100% cotton fabrics. Measurements include 1/4" seam allowances. Sew with right sides together unless otherwise stated.

Cut Fabrics

Cut pieces in the following order. Cut blue-and-green stripe outer border strips lengthwise (parallel to the selvages), centering each over the same blue stripe (Cutting Diagram).

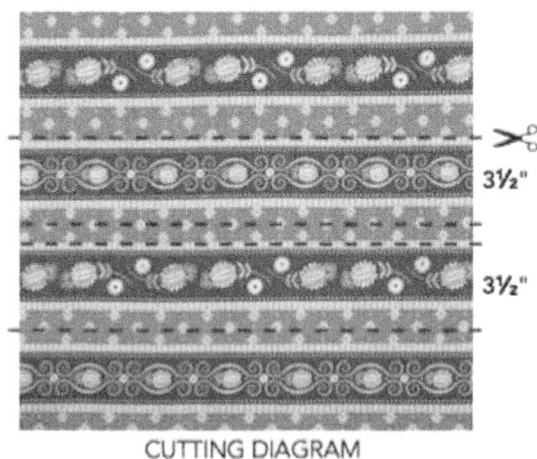

CUTTING DIAGRAM

From yellow print, cut:

3--5-3/4" squares, cutting each diagonally twice in an X to make 12 small triangles total

From solid cream, cut:

5--5-3/4" squares, cutting each diagonally twice in an X to make 20 small triangles total

36

From red print, cut:

6--5-3⁄8" squares, cutting each in half diagonally for 12 large triangles total or fussy-cut 12 of Large Triangle Pattern (3 sets of 4 matching triangles)

From green print, cut:

2--5-3⁄4" squares, cutting each diagonally twice in an X to make 8 small triangles total

From blue print, cut:

4--5-3⁄8" squares, cutting each in half diagonally for 8 large triangles total or fussy-cut 8 of Large Triangle Pattern (2 sets of 4 matching triangles)

From solid red, cut:

3--1-1/2×42" strips for inner border

From blue-and-green stripe, fussy-cut lengthwise:

2--3-1/2×61" outer border strips

2--3-1/2×25" outer border strips

From blue check, cut:

Enough 2-1/2"-wide bias strips to total 154" in length for binding

Assemble Blocks

1. For one red Pinwheel block, gather four yellow print small triangles, four solid cream small triangles, and four red print large triangles.

2. Sew together a yellow print small triangle and a solid cream small triangle to make a triangle pair. Press seam toward yellow print. Repeat to make four triangle pairs total.

3. Join a triangle pair and a red print large triangle along long edges to make a block unit. Press seam toward large triangle. The block unit should be 5" square including seam allowances. Repeat to make four block units total.

4. Referring to Diagram 1, lay out block units in pairs. Sew together units in each pair. Press seams in opposite directions. Join pairs to make a red Pinwheel block; press seam in one direction. The block should be 9-1/2" square including seam allowances.

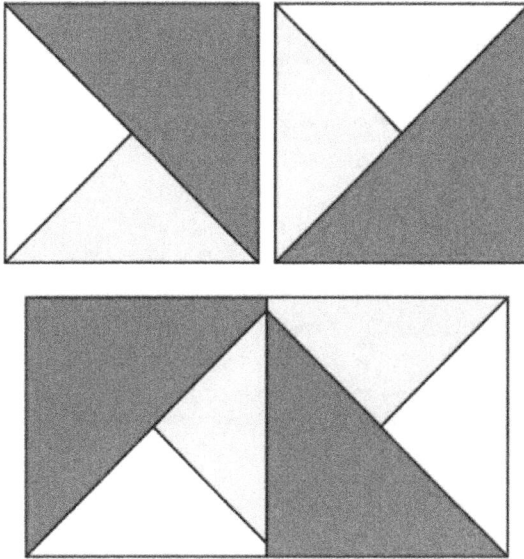

Diagram 1

5. Repeat steps 1–4 to make three red Pinwheel blocks total.

6. Using green print small triangles, remaining solid cream small triangles, and blue print large triangles, repeat steps 2–4 to make two blue Pinwheel blocks.

Assemble Table Runner Center

Referring to Table Runner Assembly Diagram, lay out blocks in a row. Join blocks to make table runner center. Press seams in one direction. The table runner center should be 9-1/2×45-1/2" including seam allowances.

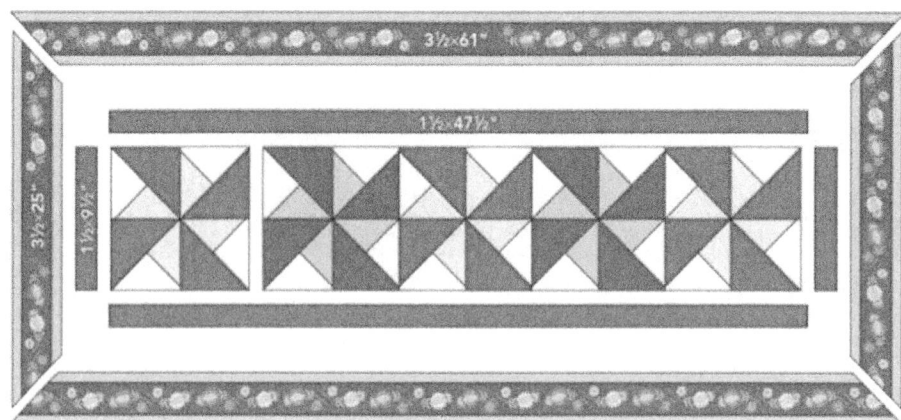

TABLE RUNNER ASSEMBLY DIAGRAM

Add Borders

1. Cut and piece solid red 1-1/2×42" strips to make:

2---1-1/2×47-1/2" inner border strips

2---1-1/2×9-1/2" inner border strips

2. Sew short inner border strips to short edges of table runner center. Add long inner border strips to remaining edges. Press all seams toward inner border.

3. Fold table runner center in half crosswise and lengthwise; finger-press lightly to mark centers of side edges. Fold each blue-and-green stripe 3-1/2×61" outer border strip in half crosswise; finger-press to mark center. Repeat to mark centers of blue-and-green stripe 3-

1/2×25" outer border strips.

4. Aligning midpoints, sew long blue-and-green stripe outer border strips to long edges of table runner center, beginning and ending seams 1/4" from corners. In same manner, sew short outer border strips to remaining edges, mitering corners, to complete table runner top. Press all seams toward outer border.

Finish Table Runner

1. Layer table runner top, batting, and backing; baste.

2. Quilt as desired. Bind with blue check bias binding strips.

Table Wear

Dress up your dinner table for summer with an easy-to-sew runner made from handy 2-1/2"-wide precut strips.

Materials

25--2-1/2×42" precut strips of assorted bright prints in teal, orange, blue, pink, and green (table runner center)

1-1/2 yards white print (border, backing)

1-1/2 yards fusible fleece (such as Pellon 987F)

Finished table runner: 16×50"

Quantities are for precut 21/2×42" strips and 44/45"-wide, 100% cotton fabrics.

Measurements include 1/4" seam allowances. Sew with right sides together unless otherwise stated.

Cut Fabrics

Cut pieces in the following order. Cut white print rectangle lengthwise (parallel to the selvages).

From each bright print strip, cut:

1--2-1/2×12-1/2" strip

From white print, cut:

1--20-1/2×50-1/2" rectangle

From fusible fleece, cut:

1--16×50" rectangle

Assemble Table Runner

1. Aligning long edges, sew together assorted bright print 2-1/2×12-1/2" strips in a row to make pieced panel (Diagram 1). Press seams in one direction. The pieced panel should be 12-1/2×50-1/2" including seam allowances.

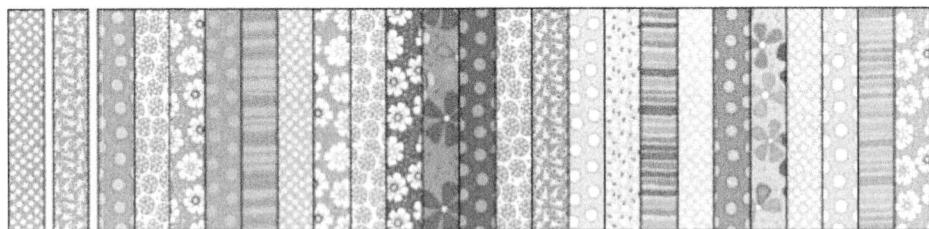

DIAGRAM 1

2. With right sides together, join pieced panel and white print 20-1/2×50-1/2" rectangle along long edges to make a tube (Diagram 2). Press seams toward white print. Do not turn right side out yet.

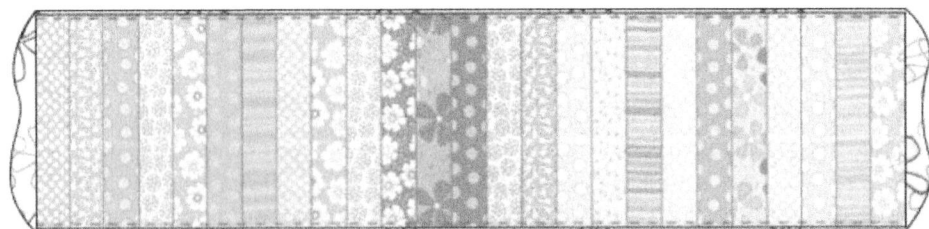

DIAGRAM 2

3. Center pieced panel on white print rectangle, allowing 2" of white print above and below panel; press (Diagram 3).

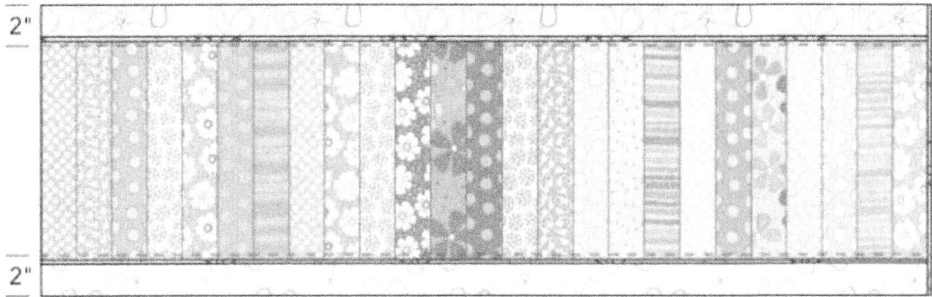

2"

2"

DIAGRAM 3

4. Turn over tube so wrong side of white print is facing up. Center 16×50" fusible fleece rectangle on tube, leaving 1/4" of white print remaining at each end. Trim fleece if needed.

5. Referring to manufacturer's instructions, fuse fleece to wrong side of tube.

6. Turn tube right side out. Press, straightening edges and smoothing wrinkles, to make long edges of table runner.

7. Turn short ends of table runner to inside 1/4"; press. Topstitch 1/8" from outer edges to complete table runner.

8. Quilt table runner as desired. Designers machine-quilted the pieced panel 1/4" on both sides of each seam.

Charming Floral Table Runner

Highlight 5" charm squares between 2-1/2"-wide fabric strips in a quilt-as-you-go table runner to make home decor in no time.

Materials

9--5" squares assorted yellow, blue, and red prints (table runner top)

3--2-1/2×42" green print strips (table runner top)

1--2-1/2×42" yellow print strip (table runner top)

3--2-1/2×42" red print strips (binding)

5/8 yard backing fabric

20×38" batting

Basting spray (optional)

Water-soluble marker

Finished table runner: 14×30"

Yardages and cutting instructions are based on 42" of usable fabric width.

Measurements include 1/4" seam allowances. Sew with right sides together unless otherwise stated.

Cut Fabrics

Cut pieces in the following order.

From assorted green prints, cut:

6--2-1/2×14" strips

From each green print and yellow print strip, cut:

2--2-1/2×14" strips

Assemble, Quilt, and Finish Table Runner

1. Lay backing fabric, right side down, on work surface. Place batting on top. If desired, use quilt basting spray to secure layers together.

2. Use a water-soluble marker to draw centered vertical and horizontal placement guidelines on quilt batting.

3. Sew together three assorted yellow, blue, and red print 5" squares in a row. Press seams in one direction. The row should be 5×14" including seam allowances. Bring short ends of row together and finger-press. Then bring long ends together; finger-press to create placement guidelines.

4. Repeat Step 3 to make three pieced rows total. Bring short ends only of two rows together and finger-press.

5. With right side up, pin a Step 3 row across middle of layered batting and backing, aligning folded placement lines on pieced row with marked placement lines (Diagram 1).

6. With RS down, place a green print 2-1/2×14" strip atop first row. Sew together through all layers (Diagram 2). Finger-press strip open.

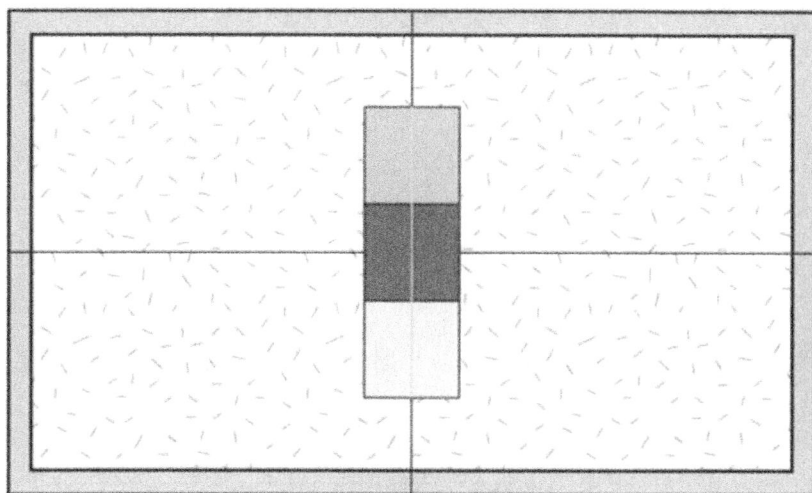

Diagram 1

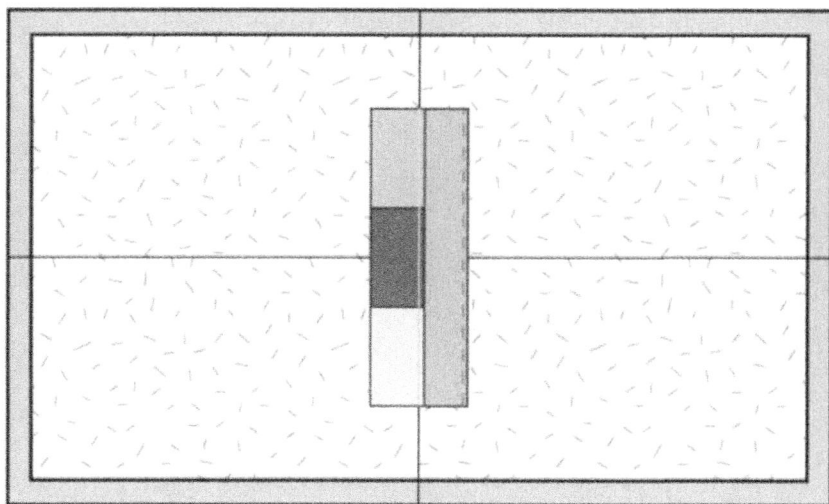

Diagram 2

7. Referring to Table Runner Assembly Diagram, continue adding assorted green and yellow print 2-1/2×14" strips and 5×14" pieced

rows in both directions to make table runner; press.

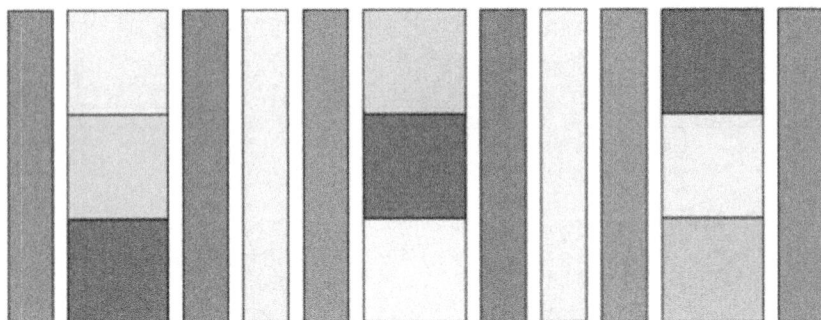

QUILT ASSEMBLY DIAGRAM

8. Trim batting and backing even with table runner top. Bind table runner with red print binding strips.

Petal Pushers

Create appliqués with a little extra pop using batting and freezer paper for a trapunto effect. Before you set the table for spring, whip up coordinating napkins.

Materials

Quantities are for table runner and four napkins.

1/4 yard multicolor dot (appliqués)

1/2 yard green polka dot (appliqués, binding)

1-7/8 yards multicolor stripe (appliqués, backing)

1/8 yard purple polka dot (appliqués)

1-7/8 yards solid white (appliqué foundation, napkin lining)

1 yard each of white-and-lavender dot and white-and-green dot (napkins)

32×66" batting

Freezer paper

Finished table runner: 16×60"

Finished napkins: 15" square

Quantities are for 44/45"-wide, 100% cotton fabrics.

Measurements include 1/4" seam allowances. Sew with right sides together unless otherwise stated.

Cut Fabrics

Cut pieces in the following order. Cut backing and appliqué foundation rectangles lengthwise (parallel to the selvages).

From multicolor dot, cut:

21 of Leaf Pattern

From green polka dot, cut:

4--2-1/2×42" binding strips

9 of Leaf Pattern

From multicolor stripe, cut:

1--22×66" backing rectangle

6 of Leaf Pattern

From purple polka dot, cut:

6 of Leaf Pattern

From solid white, cut:

1--18×62" rectangle for appliqué foundation

4--15-1/2" squares

From white-and-lavender dot, cut:

4--15-1/2" squares

From white-and-green dot, cut:

4--15-1/2" squares

From batting, cut:

1--22×66" rectangle

42 of Leaf Pattern

Prepare Appliqués

Designer used a freezer-paper method for appliquéing. To use this method, complete the following steps.

1. Layer freezer paper, shiny side down, over Leaf Pattern. Use a pencil to trace pattern 42 times, leaving at least 1/2" between shapes. Cut out freezer-paper shapes on drawn lines.

2. Center a batting piece and a freezer-paper template with shiny side up on the wrong side of multicolor dot leaf (Diagram 1).

3. Using tip of a hot dry iron, press fabric seam allowance over edge of

freezer paper, ensuring fabric is taut against template. For sharp outer points, first fold fabric straight over points of freezer-paper template (Diagram 2). Then press under remaining edges (Diagram 3). The seam allowance will adhere to the freezer paper. (Do not touch iron soleplate to freezer paper past turned fabric edge.)

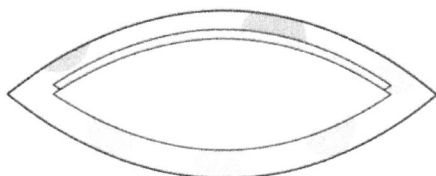

DIAGRAM 1

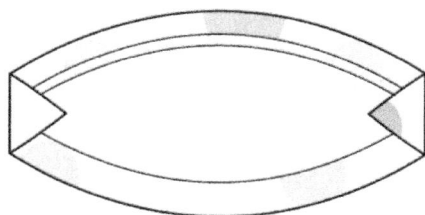

DIAGRAM 2

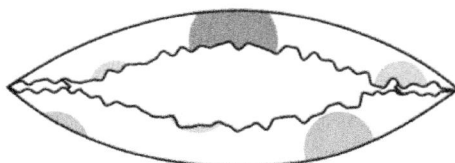

DIAGRAM 3

4. Repeat steps 2 and 3 to prepare remaining multicolor dot, green polka dot, multicolor stripe, and purple polka dot leaf appliqués.

Appliqué Table Runner Top

1. Referring to photo, position leaf appliqués on solid white 18×62" appliqué foundation in a gentle curve; pin in place.

2. Using thread that matches appliqués and a small slip-stitch, hand-appliqué around most of a leaf appliqué. Carefully peel off freezer-paper template and discard, then finish sewing around leaf. Stitch around each leaf in same manner to complete table runner top.

Finish Table Runner

1. Layer table runner top and batting and backing rectangles; baste.

2. Quilt as desired. To further enhance the trapunto effect, outline-quilted around each leaf appliqué, machine-quilted an allover swirl pattern on the remainder of the quilt top (Quilting Diagram).

3. Trim quilted table runner to 16×60" including seam allowances. Bind with green polka dot binding strips.

QUILTING DIAGRAM

Assemble Napkins

1. With right sides together, layer a white-and-lavender dot 15-1/2" square and a white-and-green dot 15-1/2" square. Place a solid white 15-1/2" square atop layered squares; press. (The third layer of solid white prevents show-through on this reversible napkin and gives it

57

more stability.)

2. Sew together around all edges, leaving an 8" opening for turning in the middle of one edge (Diagram 4). Clip across each corner. Turn right side out and press. Hand-stitch opening closed.

DIAGRAM 4

3. Topstitch 1/8" and 1" from all edges to complete napkin.

4. Repeat steps 1–3 to make four napkins total.

Star-Spangled Summer

Celebrate the season with a table runner that embraces the best of summer – watermelon.

Materials

1/4 yard white tone-on-tone (watermelon)

1/3 yard red tone-on-tone (watermelon)

1/4 yard green print (watermelon)

12" square each dark tan print No. 1 and light tan print No. 2 (background)

1/4 yard each dark tan print No. 2 and light tan print No. 1 (background)

7/8 yard navy blue tone-on-tone (border, binding)

Scrap of solid black (appliqués)

8×11" rectangle gold tone-on-tone (appliqués)

1-2/3 yards backing fabric

60×27" batting

Lightweight fusible web

Stabilizer

Finished table runner: 51-1/2×18-1/2"

Quantities are for 44/45"- wide, 100% cotton fabrics. Measurements include 1/4" seam allowances. Sew with right sides together unless otherwise stated.

Cut Fabrics

Cut pieces in the following order. To use fusible web for appliquéing patterns A and B, complete the following steps.

1. Lay fusible web, paper side up, over patterns. Use a pencil to trace each pattern the number of times indicated in cutting instructions, leaving 1/2" between tracings. Cut out each fusible-web shape roughly 1/4" outside traced lines.

2. Following manufacturer's instructions, press fusible-web shapes onto wrong sides of designated fabrics; let cool. Cut out fabric shapes on drawn lines. Peel off paper backings.

From white tone-on-tone, cut:

1--1-1/2×31-1/2" strip

2--1-1/2×8-1/2" rectangles

2--1-3/4" squares

From red tone-on-tone, cut:

1--8-1/2×31-1/2" rectangle

From green print, cut:

1--1-1/2×31-1/2" strip

2--2-1/2×8-1/2" rectangles

6--1-1/2" squares

From dark tan print No. 1, cut:

2--3-1/2×4-1/2" rectangles

2--2-1/2" squares

From dark tan print No. 2, cut:

1--1-1/2×37-1/2" strip

2--3-1/2×4-1/2" rectangles

From light tan print No. 1, cut:

1--1-1/2×31-1/2" strip

2--3-1/2×7-1/2" rectangles

2--1-1/2" squares

From light tan print No. 2, cut:

2--3-1/2×4-1/2" rectangles

From navy blue tone-on-tone, cut:

4--3-1/2×42" strips for border

4--2-1/2×42" binding strips

From solid black, cut:

10 of Pattern A

From gold tone-on-tone, cut:

6 of Pattern B

Assemble Units

1. Use a pencil to mark a diagonal line on wrong side of each white tone-on-tone 1-3/4" square, green print 1-1/2" square, dark tan print No. 1-2-1/2" square, and light tan print No. 1--1-1/2" square. (To prevent fabric from stretching as you draw lines, place 220-grit sandpaper under each square.)

2. Align a marked white tone-on-tone square with one corner of red tone-on-tone 8-1/2×31-1/2" rectangle (Diagram 1; note direction of drawn line). Sew on drawn line, then trim excess, leaving a 1/4" seam allowance. Press open attached triangle, pressing seam toward triangle.

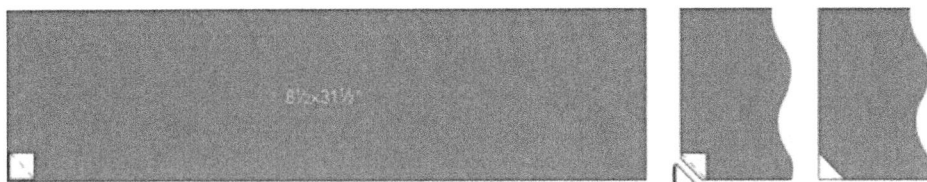

DIAGRAM 1

3. In same manner, add remaining marked white tone-on-tone square to opposite corner of red rectangle, reversing direction of drawn line. Stitch, trim, and press as before to make Unit A (Diagram 2). Unit A should be 8-1/2×31-1/2" including seam allowances.

DIAGRAM 2
UNIT A

4. Add a marked green print square to one end of a white tone-on-tone 1-1/2×8-1/2" rectangle (Diagram 3; note direction of drawn line). Stitch, trim, and press as before to make Unit B. Unit B should be 1-1/2×8-1/2" including seam allowances.

5. Repeat Step 4, reversing direction of drawn line, to make Unit B reversed (Diagram 4).

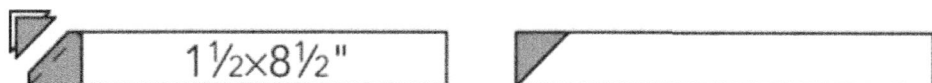

DIAGRAM 3
UNIT B

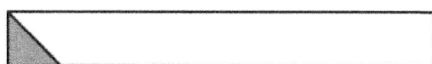

DIAGRAM 4
UNIT B reversed

6. Add a marked dark tan print No. 1 square to one end of a green print 2-1/2×8-1/2" rectangle (Diagram 5; again note direction of drawn line). Stitch, trim, and press as before to make Unit C. Unit C should be 2-1/2×8-1/2" including seam allowances.

7. Repeat Step 6, reversing direction of drawn line, to make Unit C reversed (Diagram 6).

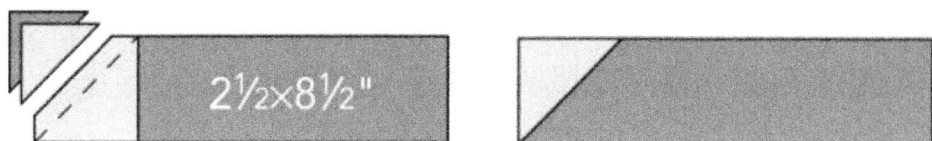

DIAGRAM 5
UNIT C

DIAGRAM 6
UNIT C reversed

8. Add a marked green print square to one end of white tone-on-tone 1-1/2×31-1/2" strip (Diagram 7; note direction of drawn line). Stitch, trim, and press as before. In same manner, add a marked green print square to opposite end of white tone-on-tone strip (again note direction of drawn line). Stitch, trim, and press as before to make Unit D (Diagram 7). Unit D should be 1-1/2×31-1/2" including seam allowances.

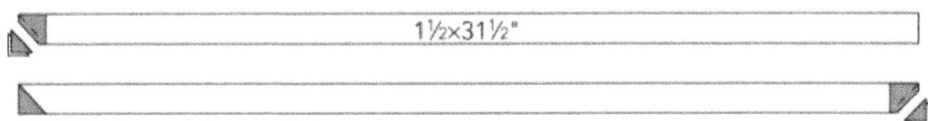

DIAGRAM 7
UNIT D

9. Using green print 1-1/2×31-1/2" strip and two marked light tan print No. 1 squares, repeat Step 8 to make Unit E (Diagram 8).

DIAGRAM 8
UNIT E

10. Add a marked green print square to one corner of a light tan print No. 1--3-1/2×7-1/2" rectangle (Diagram 9; note direction of drawn line). Stitch, trim, and press as before to make Unit F. Unit F should be 3-1/2×7-1/2" including seam allowances.

11. Repeat Step 10, reversing direction of drawn line and using

opposite end of rectangle, to make Unit F reversed (Diagram 10).

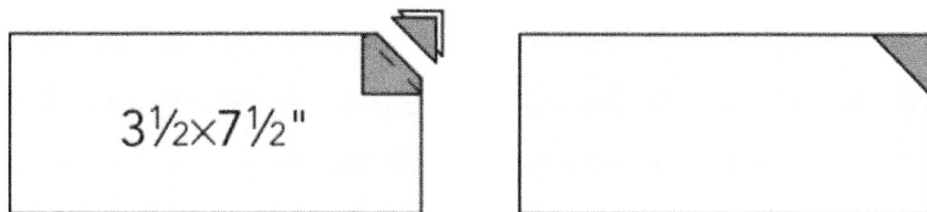

DIAGRAM 9
UNIT F

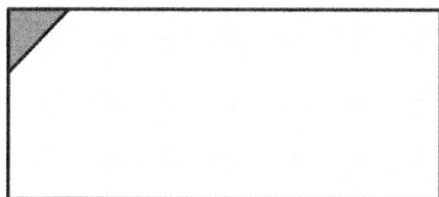

DIAGRAM 10
UNIT F reversed

12. Referring to Diagram 11, join a dark tan print No. 2--3-1/2×4-1/2" rectangle, a light tan print No. 2--3-1/2×4-1/2" rectangle, and a dark tan print No. 1--3-1/2×4-1/2" rectangle in a row to make Unit G. Press seams in one direction. Unit G should be 4-1/2×9-1/2" including seam allowances. Repeat to make a second Unit G.

3½×4½"

3½×4½"

3½×4½"

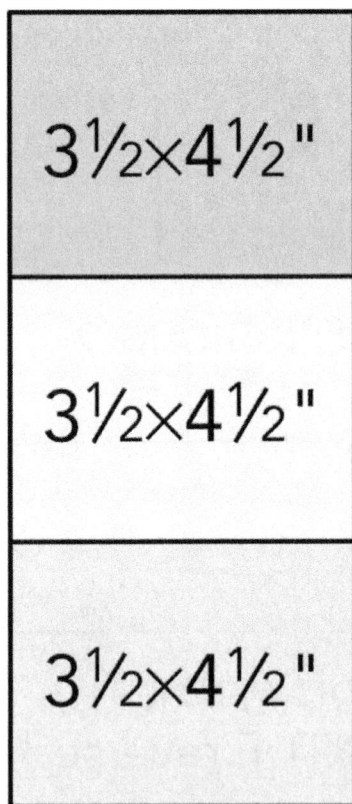

DIAGRAM 11
UNIT G

Assemble Table Runner Center

1. Referring to Table Runner Assembly Diagram, sew together units A, B, B reversed, C, and C reversed in a horizontal row. Press seams away from units B and B reversed. Sew dark tan print No. 2--1-1/2×37-

1/2" strip to top edge of the joined units. Press seam toward dark tan print strip. Add a Unit G to each side edge of joined units to make upper section. Press seams toward G units.

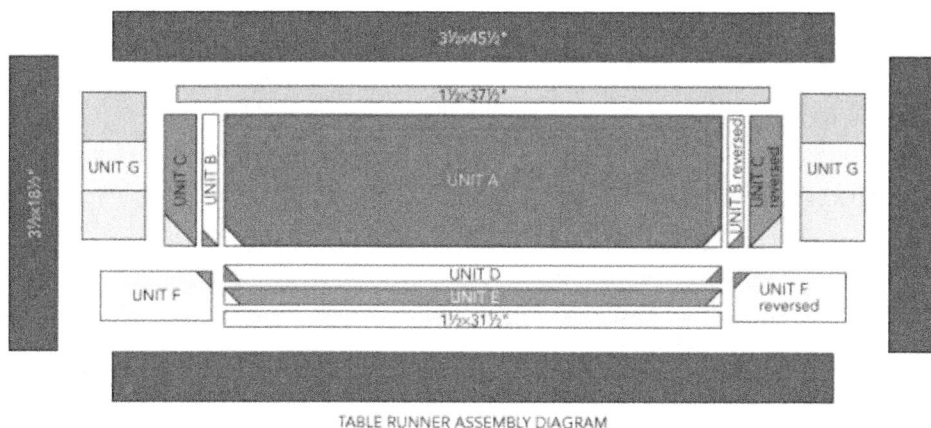

TABLE RUNNER ASSEMBLY DIAGRAM

2. Referring to Table Runner Assembly Diagram, sew together Unit D, Unit E, and light tan print No. 1--1-1/2×31-1/2" strip in a row. Press seams toward Unit E. Join Unit F to one short edge, and Unit F reversed to remaining short edge of horizontal row to make lower section. Press seams toward F units.

3. Join upper and lower sections to make table runner center. Press seam in one direction. The table runner center should be 45-1/2×12-1/2" including seam allowances.

Add Border

1. Cut and piece navy blue tone-on-tone 3-1/2×42" strips to make:

2--3-1/2×45-1/2" border strips

2--3-1/2×18-1/2" border strips

2. Sew long border strips to long edges of table runner center. Join short border strips to remaining edges to make table runner top. Press all seams toward border.

Appliqué Table Runner Top

1. Referring to photo, position solid black A seeds and gold tone-on-tone B stars on table runner top. Following manufacturer's directions, fuse in place.

2. Using matching thread, a stabilizer under table runner top, and a short stitch length (8–10 stitches per inch), machine-zigzag-stitch around edge of each appliqué to complete table runner top.

Finish Table Runner

1. Layer table runner top, batting, and backing; baste.

2. Quilt as desired. Designer machine-stitched in the ditch between each pieced section of the table runner. She used an overall stipple to add texture to the watermelon center and border, and stitched a loop motif on the watermelon rind.

3. Bind with navy blue tone-on-tone binding strips.

Patriotic Spinner Table Runner

Decorate your summer table with a quick-to-sew runner.

Materials

Yardages and cutting instructions are based on 42" of usable fabric width.

2/3 yard red star print (blocks)

1/3 yard mottled cream (blocks)

3/8 yard blue star print (blocks)

5/8 yard mottled blue (inner border, outer border, binding)

3/8 yard red, white, and blue stripe (outer border)

1-5/8 yards backing fabric

28×44" batting

Finished table runner: 23-1/2×39-1/2"

Finished block: 16" square

Cut Fabrics

Cut pieces in the following order.

From red star print, cut:

16—4-1/2" squares

64—2-1/2" squares

From mottled cream, cut:

24—2-1/2×4-1/2" rectangles

From blue star print, cut:

8—4-1/2×8-1/2" rectangles

From mottled blue, cut:

4—2-1/2×42" binding strips

4—3" squares

2—1-1/2×32-1/2" inner border strips

2—1-1/2×18-1/2" inner border strips

From red, white, and blue stripe, cut:

2—3×34-1/2" outer border strips

2—3×18-1/2" outer border strips

Assemble Blocks

Measurements include 1/4" seam allowances. Sew with right sides together unless otherwise stated.

Press seams in directions indicated by arrows on diagrams. If no direction is specified, press seam toward darker fabric.

1. Use a pencil to mark a diagonal line on wrong side of 48 red star print 2-1/2" squares and each red star print 4-1/2" square.

2. Align a marked red star print 2-1/2" square with one end of a mottled cream 2-1/2×4-1/2" rectangle (Diagram 1; note direction of marked line). Sew on marked line. Trim seam allowance to 1/4". Press open attached triangle. Add a marked red star print 2-1/2" square to

opposite end of rectangle to make a small Flying Geese unit. The unit still should be 2-1/2×4-1/2" including seam allowances. Repeat to make 24 small Flying Geese units total.

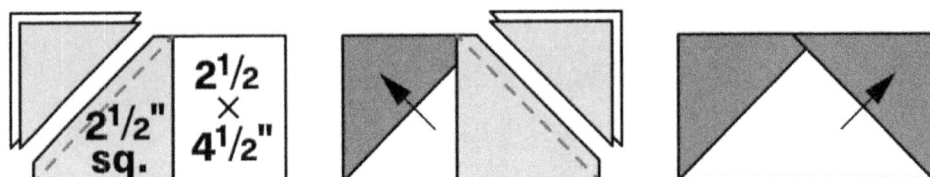

Diagram 1

3. Using marked red star print 4-1/2" squares and blue star print 4-1/2×8-1/2" rectangles, repeat Step 2 to make eight large Flying Geese units (Diagram 2). Each unit still should be 4-1/2×8-1/2" including seam allowances.

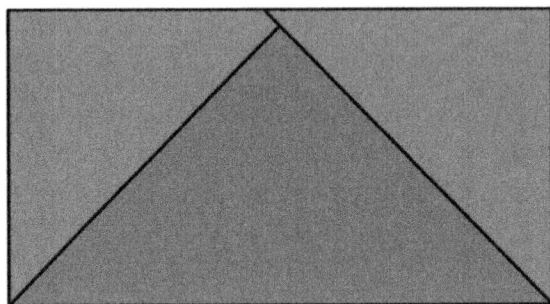

Diagram 2

4. Lay out two remaining red star print 2-1/2" squares and three small Flying Geese units in two rows (Diagram 3). Sew together pieces in

rows. Join rows to make Unit A. The unit should be 4-1/2×8-1/2" including seam allowances. Repeat to make eight A units total.

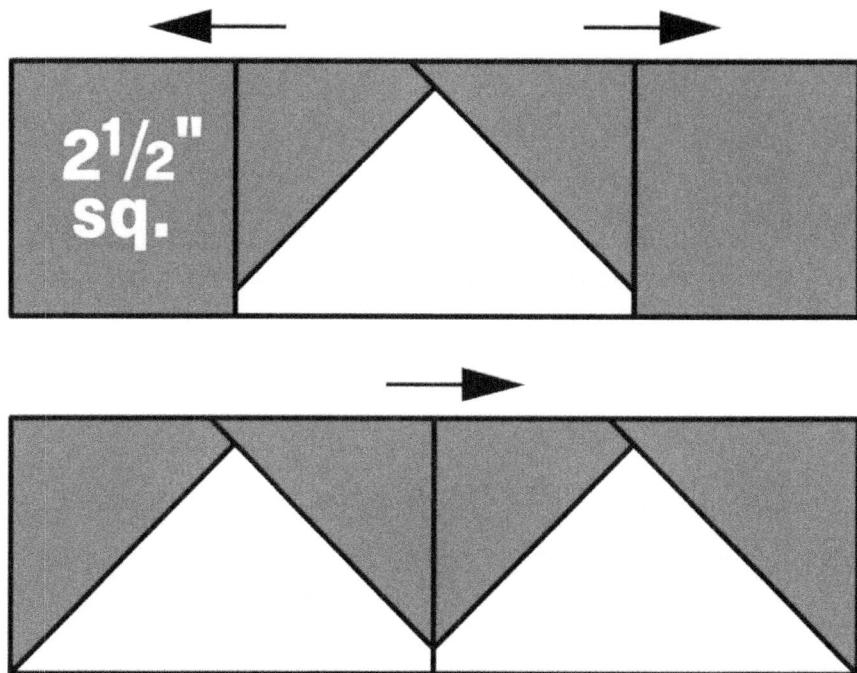

Unit A
Diagram 3

5. Referring to Diagram 4, sew together one A unit and one large Flying Geese unit to make Unit B. The unit should be 8-1/2" square including seam allowances. Repeat to make eight B units total.

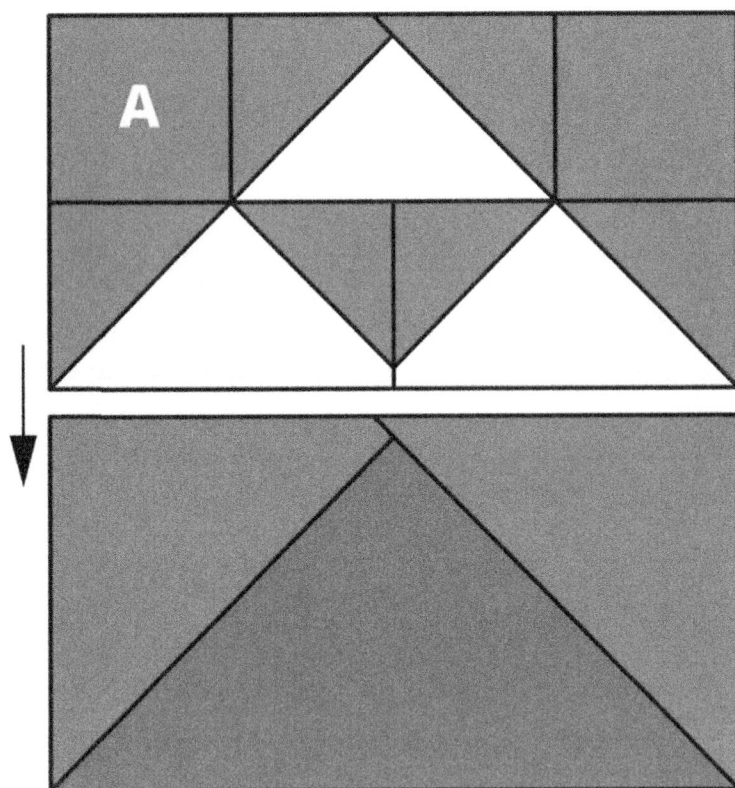

Unit B
Diagram 4

6. Referring to Diagram 5 for unit orientation, sew together four B units in pairs. Join pairs to make a block. The block should be 16-1/2" square including seam allowances. Repeat to make a second block.

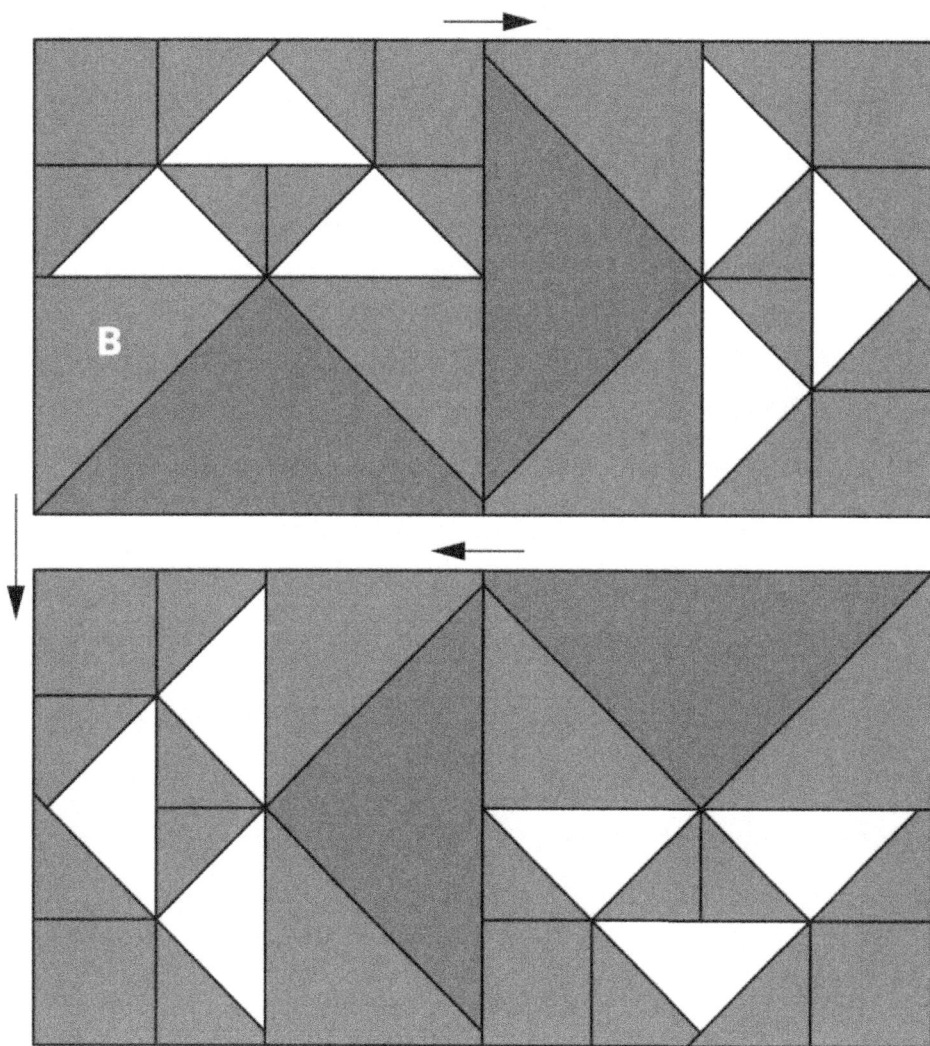

Diagram 5

Assemble Table Runner

1. Referring to Table Runner Assembly Diagram, sew blocks together.

Press seam in one direction to complete table runner center. The table runner center should be 16-1/2×32-1/2" including seam allowances.

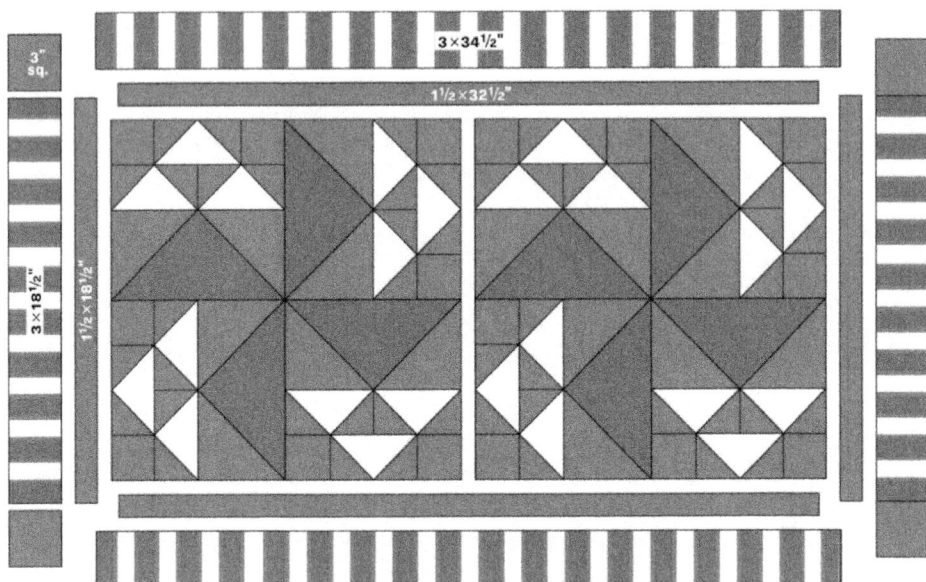

Table Runner Assembly Diagram

2. Sew mottled blue 1-1/2×32-1/2" inner border strips to long edges of table runner center. Add mottled blue 1-1/2×18-1/2" inner border strips to remaining edges. Press seams towards inner border. The table runner center should be 18-1/2×34-1/2" including seam allowances.

3. Sew together two mottled blue 3" squares and one red, white, and blue 3×18-1/2" strip to make a pieced outer border strip. The strip should be 3×23-1/2" including seam allowances. Repeat to make a second pieced outer border strip.

4. Sew red. white, and blue 3×34-1/2" outer border strips to long edges of table runner center. Add pieced outer border strips to remaining edges to complete table runner top.

Finish Table Runner

1. Layer table runner top, batting, and backing; baste. Quilt as desired.

2. Bind with mottled blue binding strips.

Candy Corn Runner

Seasonal Table Runner Quilts

Use geometric prints to form a stylized interpretation of the traditional Halloween sweet treat.

Materials

Yardages and cutting instructions are based on 42" of usable fabric width.

1/3 yard total assorted yellow prints and stripes (blocks)

1-1/2 yards black dot (blocks, setting squares, backing)

1/3 yard total assorted orange dots (blocks)

1/8 yard white tone-on-tone (blocks)

19×57" batting

3-5/8 yards 1-1/4"-wide rickrack: orange

Finished size: 13×51" (including rickrack)

Finished block: 4×6"

Cut Fabrics

Cut pieces in the following order.

From assorted yellow prints and stripes, cut:

16 of Pattern A

From block dot, cut:

1—12-1/2×50-1/2" rectangle

8—4-7/8" squares, cutting each in half diagonally for 16 large triangles total

15—4-1/2" setting squares

From assorted orange dots, cut:

16 of Pattern B

From white tone-on-tone, cut:

8—2-7/8" squares, cutting each in half diagonally for 16 small triangles total

Assemble Table Runner Top

Measurements include 1/4" seam allowances. Sew with right sides together unless otherwise stated.

Press seams in directions indicated by arrows on diagrams. If no direction is specified, press seam toward darker fabric.

1. Referring to Diagram 1, sew together a yellow print or stripe A piece and a black dot large triangle.

2. Join an orange dot B piece to the yellow A piece (Diagram 2). Add a white tone-on-tone small triangle to make a block. The block should be 4-1/2×6-1/2" including seam allowances.

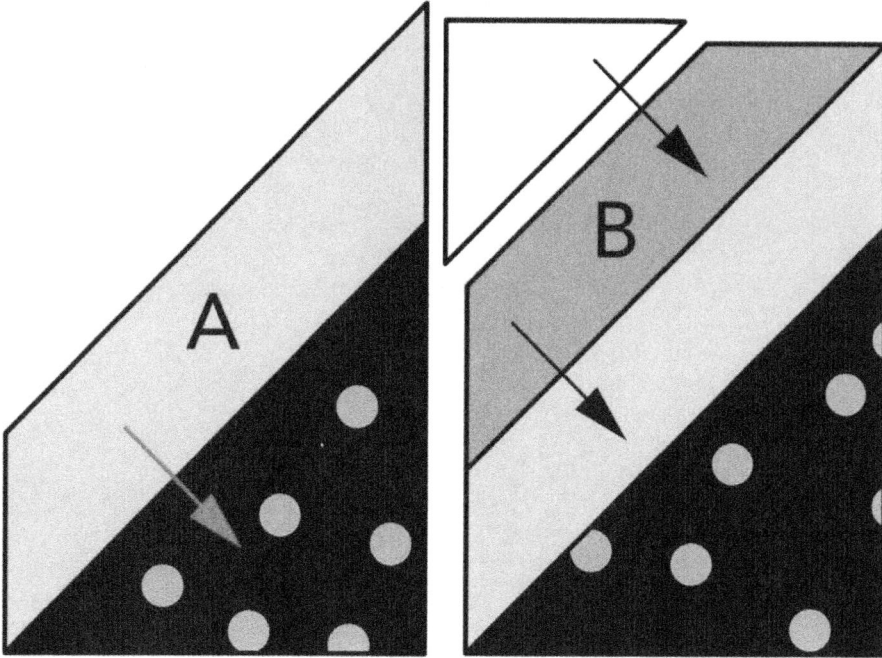

DIAGRAM 1 DIAGRAM 2

3. Repeat steps 1 and 2 to make 16 blocks total.

4. Referring to Table Runner Assembly Diagram, lay out blocks and black dot 4-1/2" setting squares in three vertical rows. The first row will extend beyond both ends of the other two rows.

TABLE RUNNER
ASSEMBLY DIAGRAM

5. Sew together pieces in each row. Press seams in one direction, alternating direction with each row. Join rows, offsetting seams as shown. Press seams in one direction. Trim first row ends even with remaining row ends to complete table runner top. The table runner top should be 12-1/2×50-1/2" including seam allowances.

Finish Table Runner

1. Pin orange rickrack to right side of table runner top, centering rickrack along edge; baste.

2. Place batting on flat surface. Center table runner top and black dot 12-1/2×50-1/2" rectangle with right sides together atop batting.

3. Sew together around all edges, leaving a 6" opening for turning. Trim batting even with table runner top and backing. Clip corners; turn right side out. Slip-stitch opening closed. Topstitch along outer edges.

4. Quilt as desired to complete table runner. Designer machine-quilted diagonal rows about 1-1/2" apart and parallel to the stripes in each "candy corn" piece.

Printed in Great Britain
by Amazon